GIANT SHARK
MEGALODON, PREHISTORIC SUPER PREDATOR

by Caroline Arnold

illustrated by Laurie Caple

CLARION BOOKS • NEW YORK

Author's acknowledgments

I would like to thank Dr. Michael Gottfried, Curator of Vertebrate Paleontology at the Michigan State University Museum, East Lansing, Michigan, for his time and expert advice. Dr. Gottfried directed the construction and installation of a life-size model of a megalodon skeleton at the Calvert Marine Museum in Solomons, Maryland. I am also grateful to the Calvert Marine Museum and Dr. Stephen J. Godfrey, Curator of Paleontology, for supplying me with information about their prehistoric shark exhibit. Special thanks go to William Celander for his photos of the exhibit.

Illustrator's acknowledgments

I am indebted to those who generously reviewed my artwork and provided expert advice on how best to depict megalodon and its world: Dr. Stephen J. Godfrey, Curator of Paleontology, Calvert Marine Museum, Solomons, Maryland; Dr. John E. McCosker and Dr. Douglas Long, California Academy of Sciences, San Francisco, California; Marie Levine, Executive Director, Shark Research Institute, Princeton, New Jersey; Dr. Malcolm Francis, Fisheries scientist, National Institute of Water and Atmospheric Research, Wellington, New Zealand; Dr. Jonathan Adams, Department of Geographical and Environmental Studies, University of Adelaide, Australia.

Many thanks to the individuals and institutions who kindly opened their facilities to me: Karsten Hartel, Harvard University Museum of Natural History, Cambridge, Massachusetts; Bonnie Davis and Dot Wensink, New England Aquarium, Boston, Massachusetts.

Special thanks to Bill Coleman of Meg MawL, Apex, North Carolina, for sharing from his collection of fossilized megalodon teeth.

Clarion Books
a Houghton Mifflin Company imprint
215 Park Avenue South, New York, NY 10003

Printed in Singapore.

Library of Congress Cataloging-in-Publication Data

Arnold, Caroline.
Giant shark : megalodon, prehistoric super predator / Caroline Arnold.
p. cm.
Summary: Describes megalodon, an extinct shark that was more than fifty feet long
and could swallow an object the size of a small car.
ISBN 0-395-91419-1
1. Carcharocles megalodon—Juvenile literature.
[1. Carcharocles megalodon. 2. Sharks.] I. Title.

QE852.L35 A76 2000   567'.3—dc21   99-086991

TWP   10 9 8 7 6 5 4 3 2 1

Contents

Megalodon

In a warm ancient sea more than 2 million years ago, a huge, deadly creature lurked beneath the waves. Propelling itself with its powerful body and tail, this enormous fish cruised the depths like a giant living torpedo. Its gaping jaws were big enough to swallow objects the size of a horse and were lined with razor-sharp teeth as big as your hand. In a single bite it could rip apart huge hunks of flesh. This fearsome predator was megalodon (MEG-uh-lo-don), the giant big-tooth shark. Now extinct, it was the biggest predatory shark that ever lived.

Bigger Than a Great White Shark

Megalodon was an enormous shark. Its body grew to be more than 50 feet long, or about the length of a large bus. It was more than twice as long as its modern relative the great white shark, which is the largest *living* predatory fish. The biggest great white shark on record measured 21 feet in length. Scientists estimate that the largest megalodon grew to at least 52 feet and perhaps longer. It would have weighed more than 105,000 pounds, or 53 tons! Since great white shark females are larger than males, it is possible that megalodon females also were larger than males and thus may have been the largest megalodons of all.

Except for its massive size, megalodon probably looked much like today's great white shark. This ocean predator is known for its compact torpedo-shaped body, big fins, and large crescent-shaped tail. Its huge mouth, which extends past its large eyes, is lined with bladelike teeth. Megalodon had a proportionately broader head and heavier lower jaw than the great white shark and more vertebrae in its backbone.

KILLER WHALE

PORBEAGLE SHARK

GREAT WHITE

MEGALODON

MAKO SHARK

SALMON SHARK

WHALE SHARK

Ancient and Modern Sharks

The first sharks were swimming in the oceans of the world 415 million years ago, long before there were dinosaurs, mammals, or birds. Sharks are among the oldest kinds of fish. Some of their basic features have changed so little over time that people sometimes think of them as living fossils. Sharks live throughout the world's oceans and play an important part in the balance of nature. Although sharks are typically viewed as dangerous predators, most species are not a threat to humans.

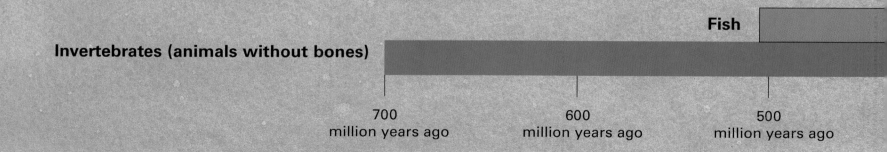

Fish

Invertebrates (animals without bones)

700
million years ago

600
million years ago

500
million years ago

Today there are about 400 living species of sharks, which are grouped in about 30 scientific families. Both megalodon and the great white shark are lamnid sharks, a family of predatory sharks that includes the mako, salmon shark, and porbeagle. This group also includes other prehistoric large-toothed sharks that were relatives of megalodon. Like megalodon, they had unusually large teeth, but none of their teeth ever reached the enormous size of those of megalodon.

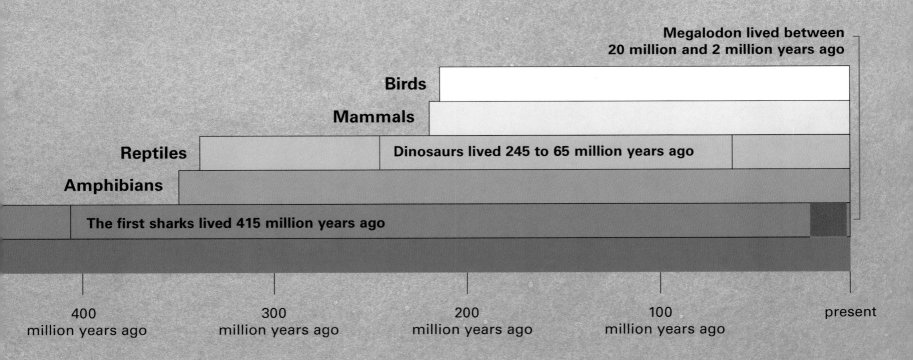

Megalodon lived between 20 million and 2 million years ago

Birds

Mammals

Reptiles

Dinosaurs lived 245 to 65 million years ago

Amphibians

The first sharks lived 415 million years ago

| 400 million years ago | 300 million years ago | 200 million years ago | 100 million years ago | present |

Megalodon's World

Megalodon roamed the oceans of the world for at least 17 or 18 million years, beginning about 20 million years ago, during a period that geologists call the Miocene Epoch. At that time, much of the Earth was covered by warm seas. The Miocene Epoch was followed by the Pliocene Epoch, which began about 5 million years ago. During the Pliocene Epoch, North and South America became joined at the Isthmus of Panama. Megalodon swam in Pliocene oceans along with ancestors of modern whales and porpoises, as well as fish and other sea life. Megalodon became extinct about 2 million years ago, near the end of the Pliocene Epoch. Although some people think megalodon may have been alive much more recently, there is no accurately dated fossil evidence to show that it was.

Although megalodon has long been gone, we know that these sharks existed because of the teeth they left behind. Giant teeth have been unearthed from hillsides in California and from fossil deposits in Florida, Maryland, and North Carolina, as well as in Belgium, Morocco, Mexico, South America, South Africa, and other places once covered by ancient seas. The biggest megalodon tooth ever found was nearly 7 inches tall. It was discovered in Peru in 1987. By comparison, the largest tooth of a great white shark is only $2\frac{1}{2}$ inches high.

Megalodon teeth are triangular, with a narrow dark section between the root and the top of the tooth. The edges are serrated, like the blade of a saw. This made them ideal for cutting through flesh.

A tooth from a living shark is white. It is made of the same material as your teeth—dentine coated with hard enamel. When a tooth becomes fossilized, the living material is usually replaced by minerals. The dentine and enamel remain intact. The color of fossilized megalodon teeth varies from beige or ocher to brown or black, depending on the mineral content of the soil in which they were buried.

Replaceable Teeth

Shark teeth are among the most commonly found fossils. All sharks lose teeth frequently—a single shark may lose thousands of teeth in its lifetime. A tooth may last only a week.

A shark's mouth is lined with several rows of teeth. The teeth are loosely fastened in the jaw and often break or simply fall out. This is never a problem for the shark, because a new tooth is always ready to take its place. A shark's replacement teeth are folded back in its jaw. They pop up into place as if they were on a conveyer belt. No matter how many teeth a shark loses, it is always prepared for its next meal.

Most megalodon teeth have been found alone, separate from other teeth that might have belonged to the same individual. In a few cases, however, a complete set of teeth has been found intact, and that helps scientists understand how the teeth were arranged in the jaw.

Megalodon had a row of 28 teeth in its upper jaw and a row of 30 in the bottom. The teeth in the upper jaw were larger than those in the lower jaw, and the biggest teeth of all were located at the front. In both the upper and lower jaws, the teeth became much smaller toward the back of the mouth. The smallest known megalodon tooth is only half an inch tall. It is the last tooth in the lower jaw.

15

Shark Fossils

Sharks have skeletons made of cartilage, the same semihard material you have in your nose and ears. Sharks belong to the class of fish called Chondrichthyes (kon-DRIK-thee-eez), from the Greek words meaning "cartilage fish." Fish with bony skeletons belong to a class with the scientific name Osteichthyes (ah-stee-IK-thee-eez), meaning "bony fish." Cartilage is tough but not as strong or durable as bone. Sharks have thick skin and many layers of muscle that help support their bodies.

A fossil is any trace or remains of ancient life. Fossils are usually formed when plant or animal material is replaced by minerals, a slow process that can take thousands of years. In most cases, only an animal's hard body parts, such as teeth and bones, become fossils. Soft body parts typically rot and disintegrate before they can fossilize. Because cartilage is too soft to fossilize well, shark skeletons are rarely preserved.

No complete fossil skeleton of megalodon has ever been found. The most complete spinal column known was unearthed in Belgium in the 1860s, when fortifications around the city of Antwerp were being built. It included about 150 vertebrae, the largest measuring about 6 inches across, and belonged to a megalodon that was nearly 30 feet long.

MEGALODON VERTEBRA
Carcharodon megalodon

FISH SKELETON
Serranus erythrogaster

MAKO SHARK JAW
Isurus oxyrinchus

SHARK SKELETON
Squalus acanthias

A Megalodon Skeleton

A shark's spinal column extends from its head to the tip of its tail. Megalodon had more than 200 vertebrae in its spine. By comparison, a great white shark has between 170 and 187 vertebrae.

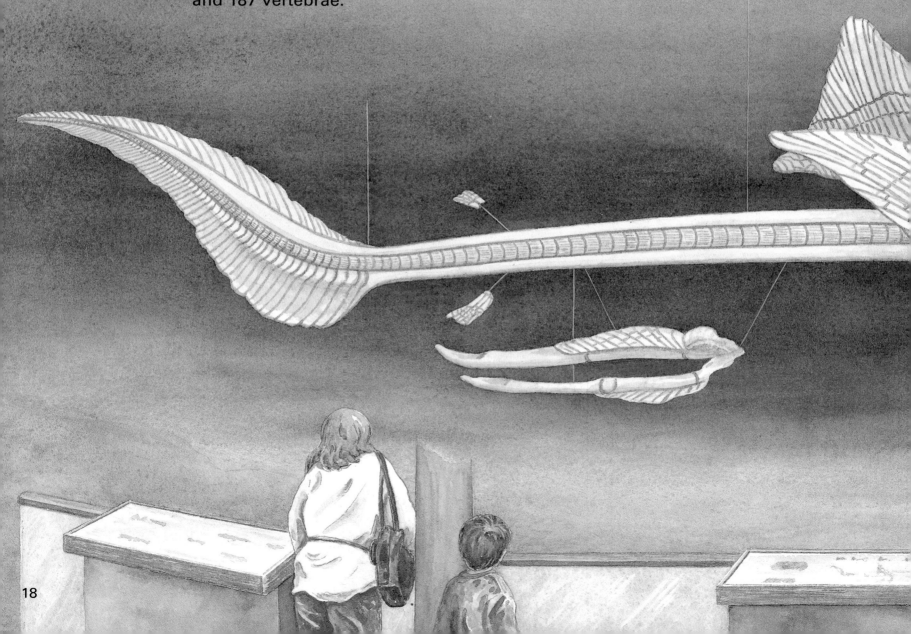

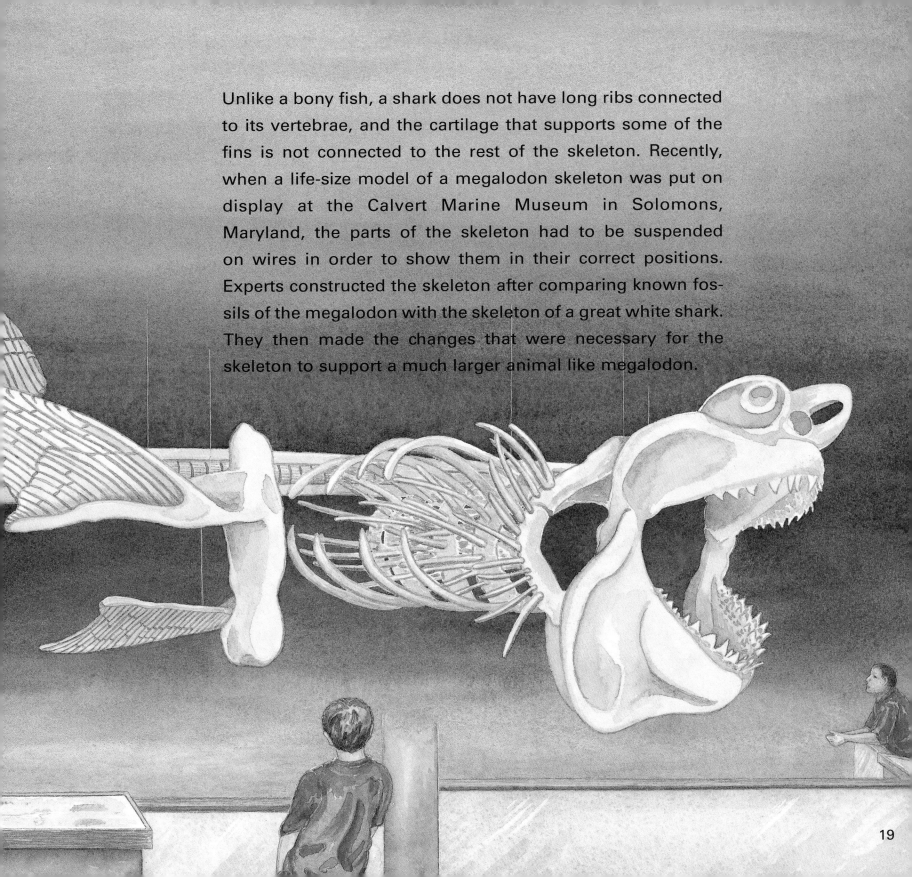

Unlike a bony fish, a shark does not have long ribs connected to its vertebrae, and the cartilage that supports some of the fins is not connected to the rest of the skeleton. Recently, when a life-size model of a megalodon skeleton was put on display at the Calvert Marine Museum in Solomons, Maryland, the parts of the skeleton had to be suspended on wires in order to show them in their correct positions. Experts constructed the skeleton after comparing known fossils of the megalodon with the skeleton of a great white shark. They then made the changes that were necessary for the skeleton to support a much larger animal like megalodon.

Inside Megalodon

No one knows exactly what the inside of a megalodon's body was like, but it probably was similar to that of other lamnid sharks Sharks swim with their mouths open. Water goes into the mouth and out the gill slits. Like other lamnid sharks, megalodon would have had five gill slits on each side of the head. Inside the gills are networks of blood vessels that absorb oxygen from the water as it passes through the gill slits. Blood is pumped across the gills by the shark's large heart. Megalodon would have needed a very large heart to circulate blood through its enormous body.

In addition to the heart, muscles, stomach, and other internal organs, sharks have unusually large livers. The liver helps in digestion. It is also important for helping to keep the shark afloat. The liver stores oil, and because oil is much lighter than water, it helps to make the shark buoyant. The great white shark's liver can be as much as one quarter of its total body weight. If we assume that the inside of megalodon was similar to the inside of a great white shark, then megalodon would have had an enormous liver, possibly weighing more than 12 tons!

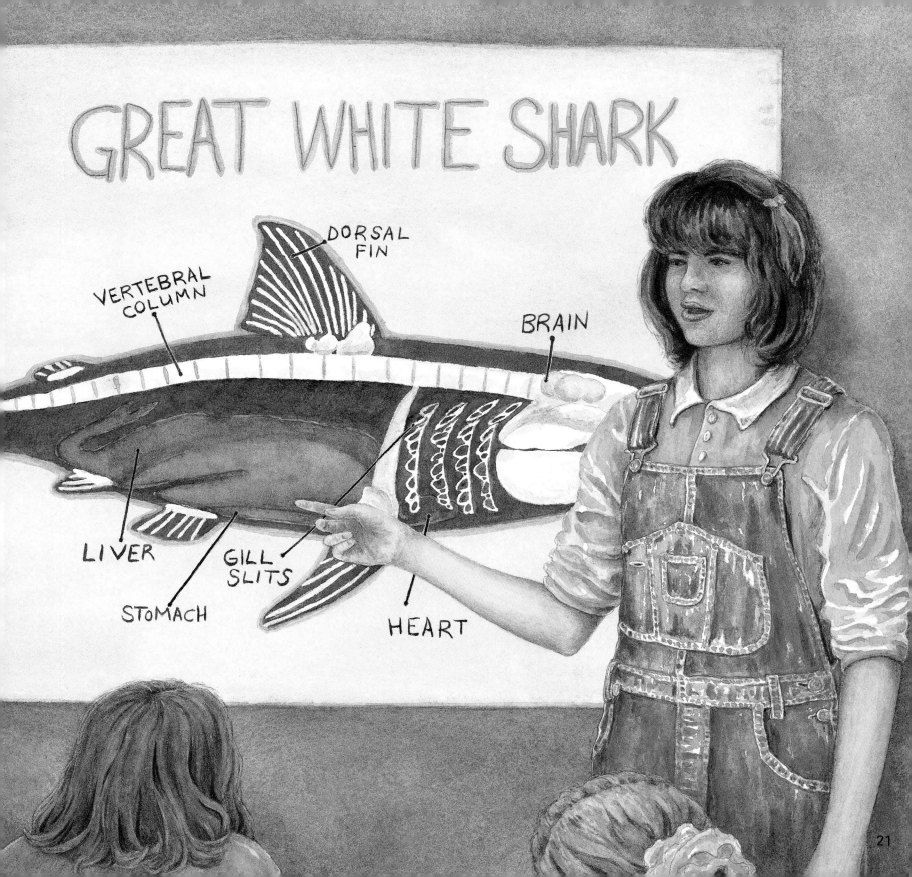

GREAT WHITE SHARK

DORSAL
FIN

VERTEBRAL
COLUMN

BRAIN

LIVER

GILL
SLITS

STOMACH

HEART

Mealtime for Megalodon

A shark as large as megalodon would have had a huge appetite. Experts believe that megalodon's main food was the meat of whales and dolphins. Fossil remains of these animals and of megalodon have been found together. In some cases, whale bones show bite marks of giant shark teeth. Although megalodon could have easily killed a large whale, it may also have fed on dead whale carcasses in the same way that great white sharks do today. Whales, dolphins, and other sea mammals have a thick layer of fat, called blubber, underneath the skin. This fat would have been a rich source of energy for a fast-swimming shark like megalodon. Megalodon probably also ate fish and smaller sea mammals, such as seals and sea lions. Like modern predatory sharks, it most likely ate whatever it could find.

Megalodon Babies

No one knows how megalodons mated and produced their young, but it is probable that they did so in the same way as other lamnid sharks. Like all fish, female lamnid sharks produce eggs, but they carry them in their bodies while the eggs are developing. Then they give birth to live baby sharks. A female megalodon may have given birth to several large babies at a time, just as the great white shark does today. A newborn great white shark is between 4 and 5 feet long and weighs about 50 pounds. By comparison, a megalodon newborn may have weighed more than 500 pounds and measured between 7 and 10 feet in length! The young megalodons would have been on their own as soon as they were born. A mother shark does not care for her offspring. In fact, she will eat them if she has a chance.

An abundance of fossils from young megalodon sharks was recently found in South Carolina. This suggests that the shallow bay that once covered that region may have been a megalodon nursery, where the young sharks lived until they grew large enough to swim in deeper waters.

What's in a Name?

Scientists classify all forms of life and give each one a two-part scientific name indicating its genus and its species. The scientific name of the great white shark is *Carcharodon carcharias* (car-CAR-o-don car-CAR-ee-us.) *Carcharodon* is the genus, and *carcharias* is the species. All members of the same genus share similar characteristics, but each combination of genus and species is unique.

Megalodon is the species name for megalodon. It comes from two Greek words: *mega,* meaning big or great, and *odon,* meaning tooth. Most scientists now studying megalodon and the great white shark think that the two sharks are so similar that megalodon should be considered as belonging to the genus *Carcharodon.* Other scientists, however, think that the two sharks are more distantly related and that megalodon should be in the genus *Carcharocles* (car-CAR-o-klays).

Although experts are able to learn much about ancient sharks just by examining their fossil teeth, it is hard to know exactly what the sharks looked like in real life. One of the difficulties of studying prehistoric life is that important evidence is often missing or incomplete. Also, some fossils may be interpreted in a variety of ways. More research is needed to resolve the conflict over the correct genus for megalodon. The debate is helping scientists better understand the ancient ancestry of sharks.

The Biggest Shark Ever?

Megalodon was the largest of the ancient predatory sharks. But was it the biggest shark that ever lived? Scientists believe that megalodon grew to be at least 52 feet long. But that is not as large as the whale shark, an enormous modern fish that grows to 60 feet and may weigh up to 20 tons. The whale shark is the largest living fish. This slow-swimming giant feeds on tiny plankton, squid, and small fish that it strains through sievelike gills. Unlike some of its predatory relatives, it is harmless to people and other large animals in the ocean.

Megalodon may have grown larger than a whale shark, but we don't know that for sure. We do know that it is the largest ocean *predator* that ever lived.

Why Did Megalodon Disappear?

Megalodon became extinct about 2 million years ago. This was just before the beginning of a major ice age, the Pleistocene Epoch, a time when the Earth was cooling and much of the land and water was becoming covered with snow and ice. No one knows exactly why megalodon disappeared. Scientists think that one of the reasons could be that its food became scarce and harder to catch. Over time the large whales that were megalodon's food had become better swimmers and could more easily get away. The whales also began to spend more time in Arctic and Antarctic waters, where fish and other foods were plentiful. Whales have thick blubber to keep them warm, but megalodon could not survive in the icy waters at the North and South Poles.

Another possible reason for megalodon's extinction may be that orcas, or killer whales, had begun to hunt in the same places as megalodon and were more successful at catching available prey. After the orcas had finished eating, there may not have been anything left for megalodon to catch.

Much of megalodon's life will always remain a mystery. But one thing that we can be sure of is that this enormous prehistoric predator was the deadliest shark ever. No creature was safe when megalodon was around. Now that megalodon is extinct, ocean dwellers no longer have to watch out for this amazing giant shark that was once the supreme hunter of the sea.